MW01657238

SUCCESS LIBRARY

THE PSYCHOLOGY OF WINNING FOR THE 21ST CENTURY

by Denis Waitley

Time never stops to rest, never hesitates, never looks forward or backward. Life's raw material spends itself now, this moment – which is why how you spend your time is far more important than all the material possessions you may own or positions you may attain.

The new millennium gives us new opportunities to evaluate what we have done in the past and what we wish to accomplish in the future. Only the actions we take here and now to plan our life's strategy can create a winning future. Make today, your moment of truth, your time to focus on a new era of opportunity.

Graphics by Balance Design

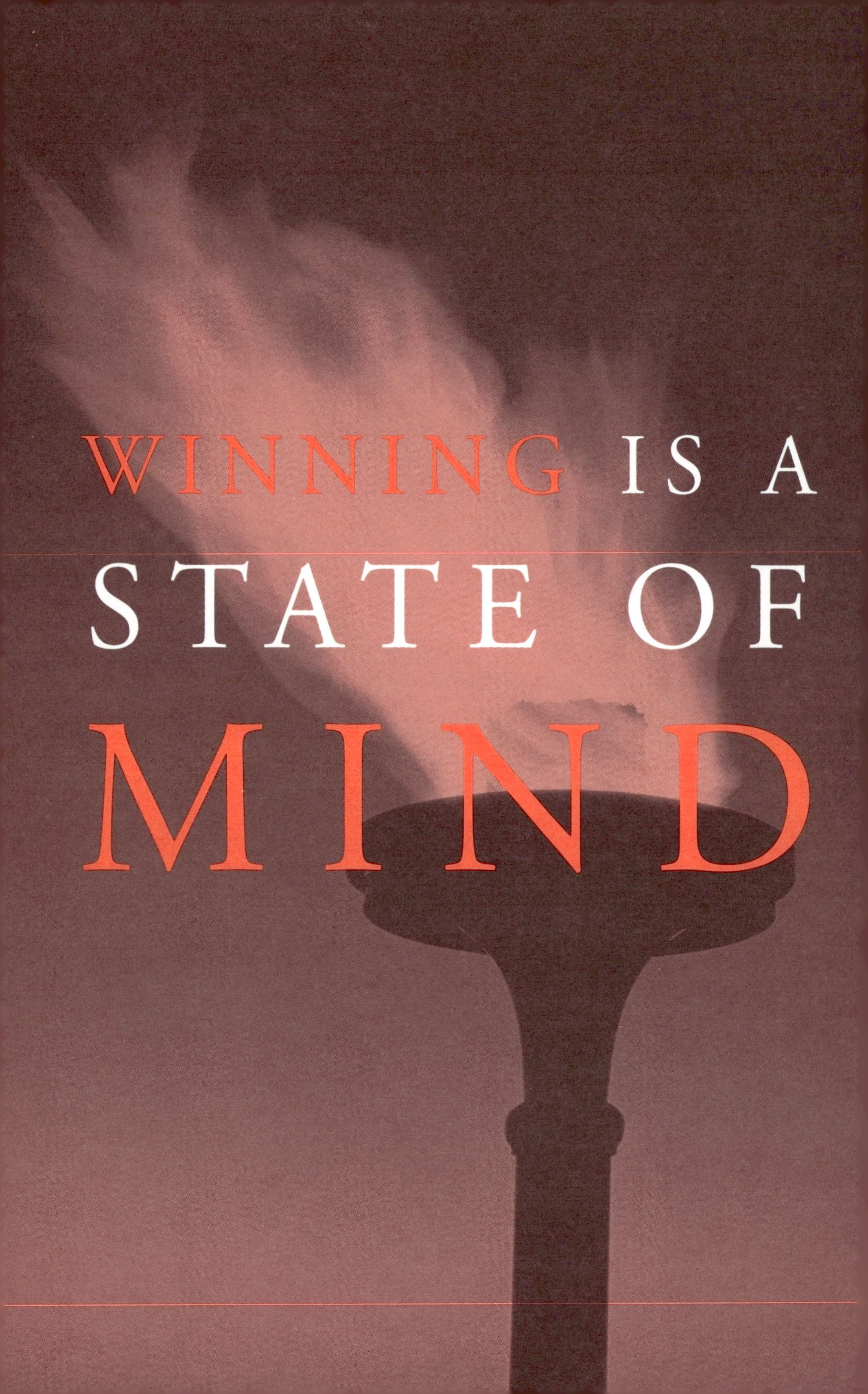
WINNING IS A
STATE OF
MIND

In order to gain the respect of others, we must first earn it. We must be respectable. In order to be a role model, we must first set a positive example. In order to lead others, we must first lead ourselves.

We must ask ourselves who is responsible for our success or failure. We need to challenge our time-worn assumptions and prejudices and reflect on the vast potential within.

Our self-esteem, self-image, and self-confidence can drag us down or carry us to the top depending upon the perspective we possess.

Self-esteem – Perhaps the most important human quality, is the deep-down, inside-the-soul feeling of your own worth, regardless of your current status. Self-esteem is a belief that you deserve to be happy and successful, combined with a trust in your ability to manage life's challenges.

Self-image – It's not "what you are" that holds you back, it's "what you think you are not." Individuals behave, not in accordance with reality, but in accordance with their perception of reality. How the individual feels about himself or herself is everything, for all that he or she ever does or aspires to be will be predicated on that all-important concept which is the self-image.

Self-confidence – Self-confidence is not just believing you can succeed, it is believing you can come back and win after you have failed, lost or been rejected.

At the world class level, talent is nearly equal. On the PGA tour only a few shots for the year separate the top money winners in golf from the rest of the players. In baseball, the American and National League batting champions hit safely about 20 or 30 more times in an entire season than those below the top ten. In the Olympic Games, the difference between the gold-medal winner in the 100-meter dash and the fourth place, non-medal winner is less than two-tenths of a second.

What's true in sports is also true in our business and personal lives. There is only a fractional difference between winners in life and those who merely exist. The difference is attitude under pressure. It's the Winner's Edge.

The Edge is not a gifted birth. The world is full of wasted talent.

The Edge is not academic degrees. Education is important, but the world is full of educated misfits.

The Edge is not luck. If it were Las Vegas would be a ghost town.

The Edge is not capital. Many of today's self-made, multi-millionaires started building their fortunes with under $5,000.

The Winner's Edge is all attitude. Attitude, not aptitude, is the criterion for success.

In the 21st century, you will be paid and promoted based on the value of your "human capital," which includes knowledge, skills, experience, creativity, adaptability and desire; not on your past education, resume, seniority or position. Becoming the "brand of choice" requires confidence in your potential and dedication to continuous improvement.

How do you perceive yourself?	*Negative*									*Positive*
Self-esteem (potential for future success)	1	2	3	4	5	6	7	8	9	10
Self-image (how you present yourself)	1	2	3	4	5	6	7	8	9	10
Self-confidence (ability and skill level)	1	2	3	4	5	6	7	8	9	10

List an activity you will do each day to improve your state of mind.

1. Self-esteem – ______________________________

____

2. Self-image – ______________________________

____

3. Self-confidence – ______________________________

____

Action Thought:
Winning is a state of mind, that even though you're far behind and though you've fallen off the pace, somehow, some way, you'll win the race!

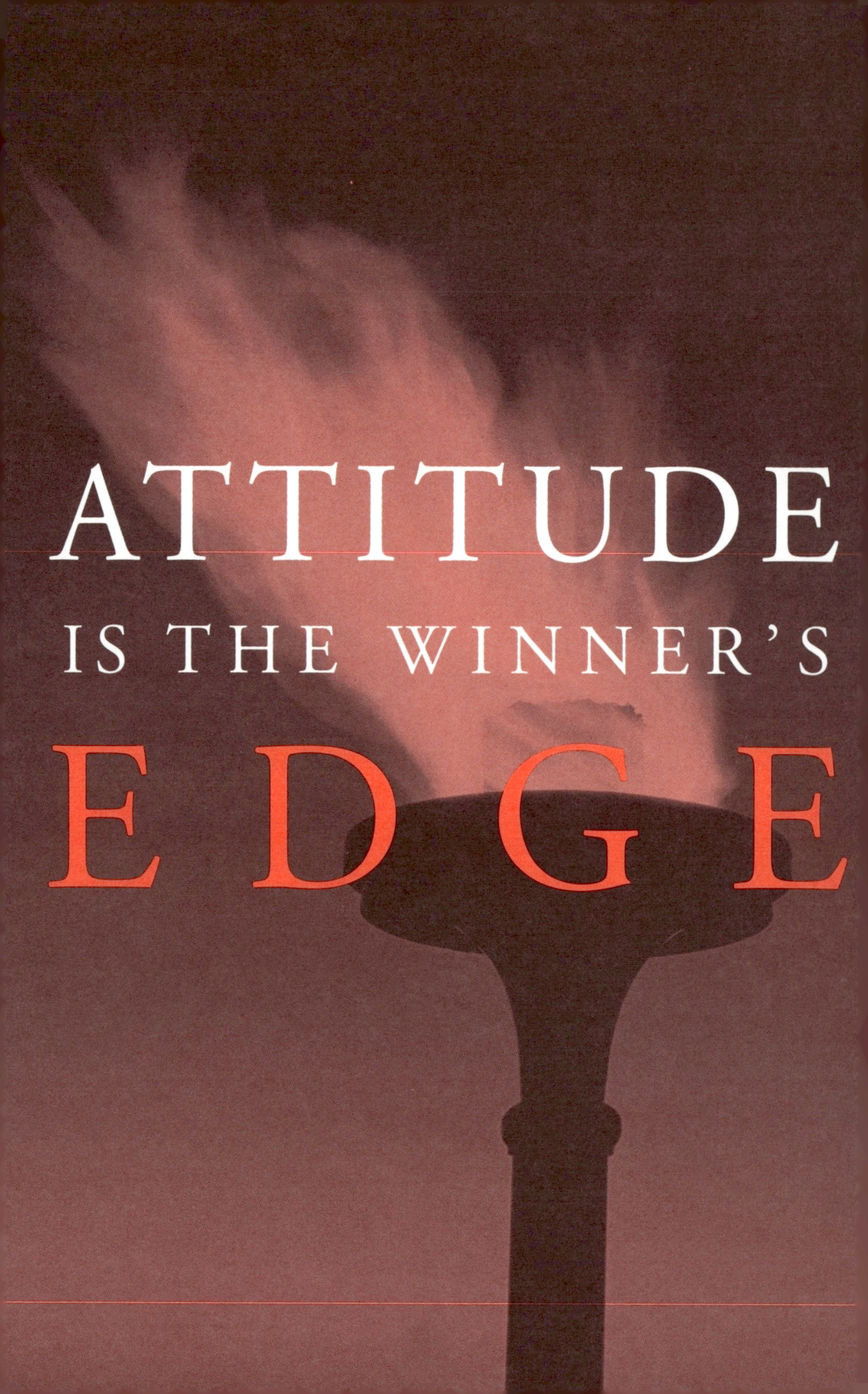

ATTITUDE IS THE WINNER'S EDGE

How you approach challenges and problems on a daily basis is a critical aspect of your decision-making process, whether in business or in your personal life. One of the most desirable attitudes of a winner is the ability to remain optimistic in uncertain times and to see challenges as opportunities, setbacks as temporary inconveniences. The positive attitude also welcomes change as friendly, and is not upset by surprises.

Two key emotions dominate human motivation with opposite, but equally effective results – fear and desire. Fear of failure is the most powerful negative motivator. It is like a hammer or red light. Fear restricts, closes, panics, forces, and ultimately abandons plans and defeats goals. Desire is like a strong, positive manager. It attracts, reaches, opens, directs, and encourages plans and achieves goals.

You will be motivated to go after any goal if you passionately believe you deserve and expect to be able to achieve it. How you prepare for success is crucial. Preparation bolsters positive expectation.

You may not get what you want in life, but in the long run, you probably will get what you expect.

In the 1920s, when an author was working hard to perfect his craft, he lost a suitcase containing all his manuscripts – many stories he'd laboriously polished to jewel-like perfection – which he'd been planning to publish as a book. The devastated writer couldn't conceive of redoing his work. He could only think of the months he'd devoted to his arduous writing – and for nothing.

But when he lamented his loss to the poet Ezra Pound, Pound called it a stroke of good luck! Pound assured him that when he rewrote the stories, he would forget the weak parts; only the best material would reappear. Instead of framing the event in disappointment, Pound cast it in the light of opportunity.

Ernest Hemingway did rewrite the stories – and the rest, as they say, is history. He became one of the major figures in American Literature.

For those seeking opportunity and creativity, the new millennium will be the best of times. In a world of constant change and uncertainty, fear of the unknown will cause many people to procrastinate and react to outcomes. Winners cause their own outcomes by gaining knowledge and being proactive.

What important but unpleasant tasks have you been delaying that require action?

____

____

____

What action steps can you put on your "to do" list for tomorrow to gain a resolution?

____

____

____

____

Action Thought:
The winner's edge is all in the attitude.
Attitude, not aptitude, is the criterion for success.

WINNERS ALWAYS
FOCUS

An individual with focused goals is very much like a laser beam. When light beams are concentrated and in step they produce energy with incredible power. A laser can execute a variety of spectacular tasks, from performing delicate eye surgery to carrying more than a hundred thousand times more information than a telephone line. It can drill through substances as hard as a diamond or soft as rubber.

The reason most individuals don't reach their goals is that they never really set them in the first place. It's obvious that the majority of people spend more time planning a party or vacation than they do planning their lives. By failing to plan, they actually are planning to fail by default. When goals are clearly defined and stair-stepped, they ignite the human mind's awesome creativity and powers of accomplishment, cutting through any obstacles encountered.

The mind is like a missile guidance system. Once a goal is set with conviction, the mind makes every correction necessary to hit the target. Filled with vague directions, the mind wanders aimlessly and misses the destination or self-destructs, using some form of rationalization and sensual gratification to mask the sense of failure.

As a boy in Scottsdale, Arizona he liked to shoot 8-mm films featuring "ordinary people pursued by large forces." He was his own writer, director and star – and he knew that this was what he wanted to do for the rest of his life, but on a larger scale. He wasn't very focused in school and there seemed to be no point in going to college. Movies, after all, were made in Hollywood, so that's where he went.

Dressed in a suit, carrying a briefcase, and looking like he belonged, he would sneak past the guards at the entrances to the major studio lots and spend the day just walking around, soaking up the atmosphere. Eventually, one of his short films gained some attention – and today, of course, Stephen Speilberg has directed half a dozen of the most profitable films ever made.

As the CEO of your own life, in the 21st Century, you need a clear vision of what your future looks like. You need a mission statement describing how you want to live, not just what you want to own. You need to define the person you want to become, not just the title you want to see on your door. Frame your mission statement starting with your core values before working outward to your material desires, tangible needs and financial objectives.

Are you doing what you want to do and becoming who you want to become?

What do your really imagine for your future?

Is it your vision or someone else's? If it is someone else's, do you share it passionately?

Action Thought:
Ensure that "You, Inc." has the habits and skills necessary to compete in the global marketplace. By becoming the CEO of your own life, you won't have to worry about being "down-sized" or "out-sourced ."

WINNERS TAKE
RISKS

As children, we either accepted or rejected the environmental "uniforms" handed to us by our parents and other significant role models. As teenagers and young adults, some of us had a strong need to conform to the standards of our peers or the entertainment media. While we fooled ourselves into thinking we were being "different," we actually were as regimented as any army calling the step and marching in full dress uniform.

Step out of your comfort zone. We are not only self-incarcerated victims of our own fears, we are victims of habit and group conformity. In a very real sense, each of us becomes a hostage of our own restrictions.

The greatest risk in life is to wait for and depend upon others for your security. The greatest security is to plan and act and take the risk that will set you free. Be different, if it means higher personal and professional standards of behavior. Be different, if it means putting more time and effort into all you do. Be different, if it means getting out of your comfort zone and daring to take the calculated risk.

Winners abandon assumptions and are open to alternatives. They are not afraid to take risks.

"The telephone is inherently of no value to us."
– Western Union, 1876

"The wireless music box (radio) has no imaginable commercial value. Who would pay for a message sent to no one in particular?"
– RCA staff, 1921

"Who the h--- wants to hear actors talk?"
– Warner Brothers, (reaction to talking movie pilot) 1929

"Stocks have reached what looks like a permanently high plateau."
– Irving Fisher, Professor of Economics, Yale, 1929

"I think there's a world market for about five computers."
– Thomas J. Watson, founder of IBM, 1950

"We don't like their sound and guitar music is on the way out."
– Decca Records (rejecting The Beatles), 1962

"There is no reason for any individual to have a computer in his or her home." – Ken Olsen, president, Digital Equipment Company, 1977

The new century will bring ample opportunity for progress. These chances for advancement will not be realized without taking a leap ahead. You must see risk as a chance for a positive change. Take risks when they come and you will ride the wave of the future.

Identify a time you took a risk to pursue something you believed in, in spite of what the majority chose.

___

___

What would you attempt to do today, if you knew you could not fail?

___

___

Who do you know that has successfully accomplished taking a risk?

___

___

Action Thought:
Welcome change as your friend. Be flexible in the face of daily surprises. Unhook prejudices. Abandon assumptions, while holding on to your core and spiritual values.

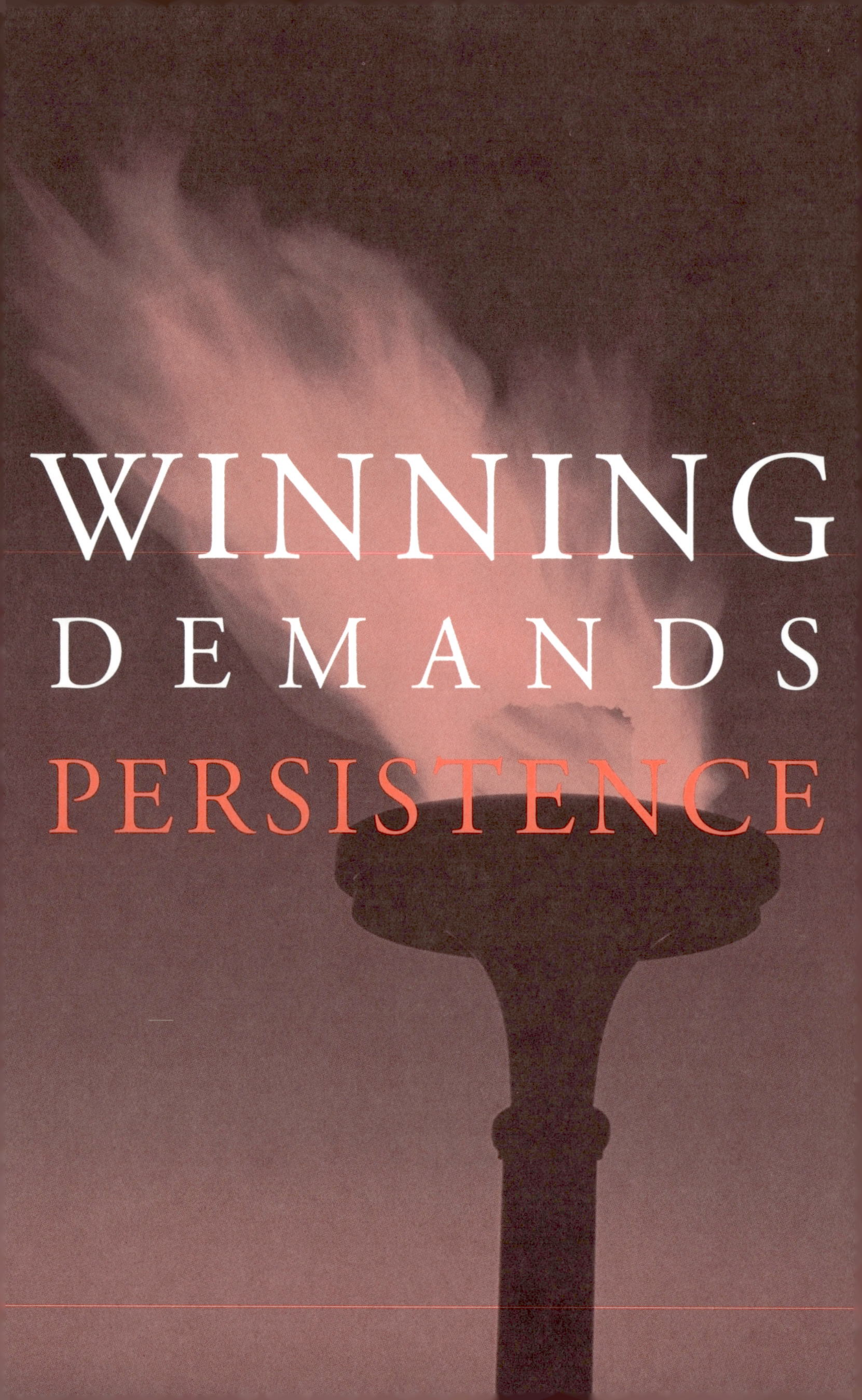
WINNING
DEMANDS
PERSISTENCE

Winners work at doing things the majority of the population is not willing to do.

A $60 per week laundry worker spent his nights and weekends for two years typing manuscripts to send to publishers and agents. Each one was rejected with a form letter. Finally, a more encouraging rejection letter arrived. It said that although his writing was not yet worthy of publishing, he should keep trying.

After two more years of rejection, finances got so tight for this young man and his wife that they had to disconnect their phone to pay for their baby's medicine. Totally discouraged, he threw his latest work in the garbage. But his wife, still believing and committed, rescued the manuscript and submitted it one last time to another publisher. The book, "Carrie," sold over five million copies and became the top box office movie the next year. The laundry worker, of course, was Stephen King.

Show me someone who has succeeded in the face of incredible odds, and I will show you a person who knows that perseverance makes the difference. It takes persistence and patience to build lasting success. Winning is hanging in there when times are tough and the odds are stacked against you. Prevailing is about sustaining, not complaining.

A young man on a bicycle is speeding along the roads of France. Greg LeMond is racing toward Paris with thirty shotgun pellets in his body. Two of them are in his heart.

Two years before he had been accidentally shot on a hunting trip. His philosophy is, "It's ten percent talent and ninety percent guts and determination." All this made Greg LeMond a superstar. He'd already won the Tour de France in 1986, the first person outside Europe ever to win this great race.

Out of action for a year, he suffered more physical setbacks both of which required surgery. Rusty and not in top shape, LeMond starts the last day of competition for the 1989 event fifty seconds behind the leader, Laurent Fignon of France. The final leg is just twenty-four kilometers, or about fifteen miles – too short a distance for LeMond to have a chance of catching Fignon. The French are already celebrating. Fignon is a certain winner. The Paris newspapers have predicted victory for the Frenchman.

Suddenly, LeMond is going faster and faster. No one can believe what's happening. You can't gain ground that fast. But he's doing it. His concentration is all-consuming, totally focused on what he's doing, willing his way to victory.

Now he's in Paris. He passes the Champs-Elysees, then the Arc de Triomphe. He streaks across the finish line. And Greg LeMond wins the Tour de France by scarcely the length of a bicycle.

While persistence is determination to achieve at all costs, patience is our umbrella when external circumstances rain on our efforts. When a goal is distant and difficult to reach, patience gives us the will to hang on. When you plant a flower, persistence keeps you digging and watering, while patience lets it grow. As with life, we cannot choose the day or time it will fully blossom. It happens in its own time.

Do you complete what you start? Always. Usually. Eventually.

When you become discouraged, what do you do to stay motivated?

How have you converted stumbling blocks in your path, into stepping stones to success? List three of your experiences.

Action Thought:
Persistence is holding your ground when you'd rather run,
counting to ten when you'd rather get mad,
keeping a smile when you'd rather cave in, and
hanging in when you'd rather give up.

WINNING TAKES
TEAMWORK

We all know that competition provides the soil in which free enterprise takes root. And we all know what happens when a company or group has no competition; there is no incentive for quality or service. However, a look at the word *compete* is revealing. It comes from the Latin source *competere,* meaning "to come together, agree, belong." Although someone does come in first, the best approach to competition is that everyone is better off just for having run the race.

Winning used to mean beating others and being Number One. It signified standing victoriously over a fallen adversary. It is obvious the very nature of "winning" must change.

The real winners in the future world arena will be more often the champions of "cooperation," rather than the champions of "competition." While power to maintain access to markets and secure world peace will continue, "the survival of the fittest" philosophy will give way to the "survival of the wisest" philosophy of understanding, sharing and reason.

Instant satellite and internet communications have created a small, global village with blurred borders and few secrets. There are too many people, too few resources, and too delicate a balance between nature and technology to produce winners in isolation today.

Back in 1994, the American Midwest suffered the most disastrous floods of the century. As the swollen rivers broke the dams, citizens rallied to save entire communities. They filled sandbags day and night, trying desperately to preserve homes, schools and businesses. These volunteers found themselves with the unlikely help of convicts from an Illinois prison system. Convicts and townspeople worked side by side to save the little town of Inota.

Many were amazed at the efforts the convicts made. They refused to stop working long enough to eat or sleep. They pressed on around the clock to stay the waters, but despite their valiant efforts the levee gave way, and the town of Inota and its two hundred homes were destroyed.

The prisoners wept, expressing their sadness and condolences to those who had lost their homes and belongings. What an amazing turn around from begrudging convicts on a forced labor project to good Samaritans with compassion for people they had never met.

For most of them, it was the first time in their lives they had experienced the feelings of working together for a worthy cause.

We must face the new millennium with the inescapable fact that we, as individuals, are a vital but single organ of a larger body of human beings in the world. The one cannot succeed, or even survive for long anymore, without the other.

Who among your contacts are your best "sounding boards?"

Think of the people you work with or see often who you know little about. How can you learn more about them? How can you benefit from their experiences?

Action Thought:
If you share yourself with others, you can reach your destination more quickly and easily because you are traveling on the power created through teamwork.

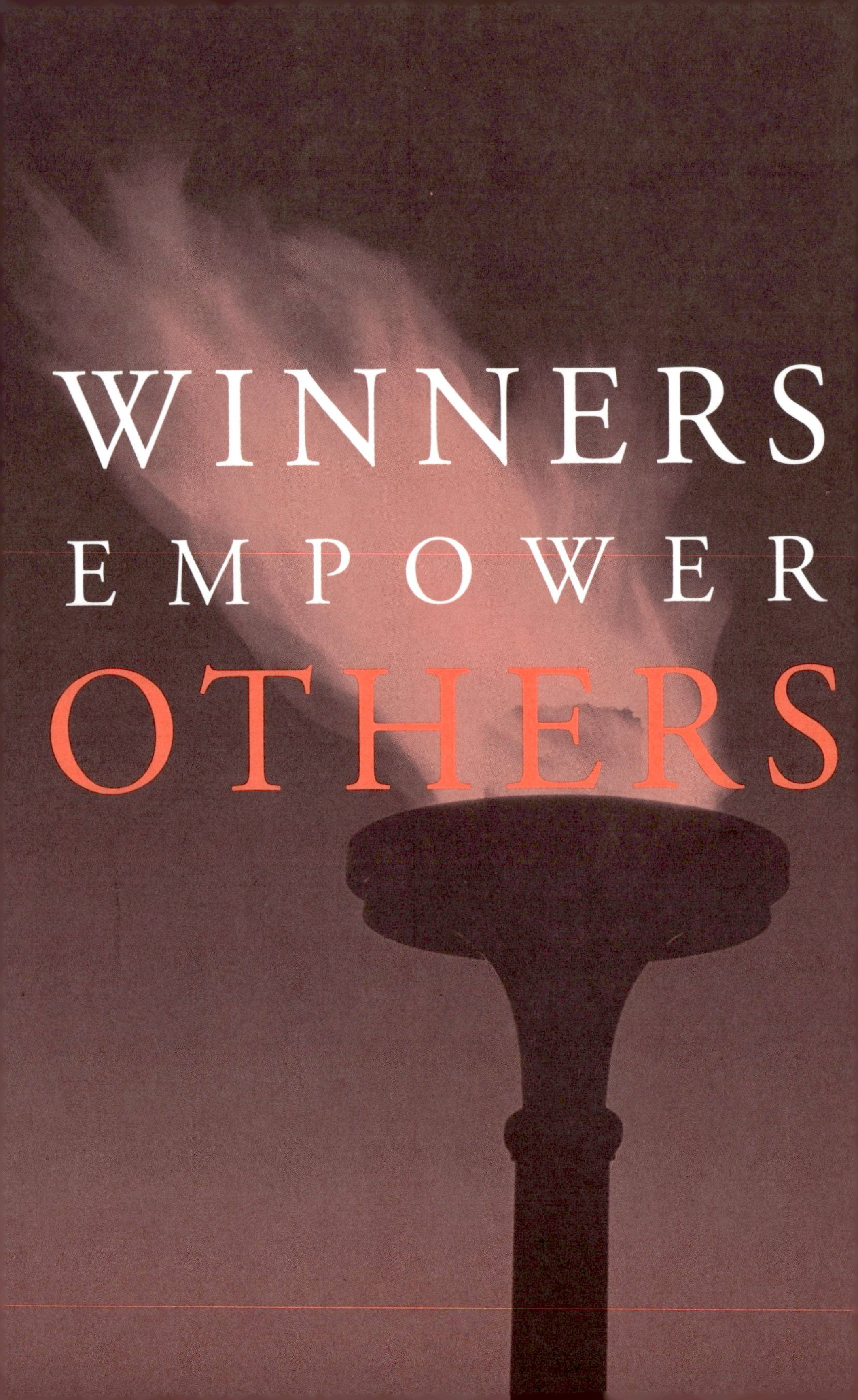
WINNERS
EMPOWER
OTHERS

The foundation of real leadership is empowerment, which is the desire to understand the needs of the people who are depending upon you, and the ability to create an environment in which they themselves can fulfill those needs.

Jack Welch, CEO of General Electric, (consistently named by business leaders as one of the most admired companies in the world) believes if we are going to satisfy customers and win in the marketplace, managers have got to simplify more, delegate more and trust more. We need to drive self-confidence deep into the organization. A company can't distribute self-confidence, but it can foster it by removing layers and giving people a chance to win.

We have to undo a 100-year-old concept of leadership and convince our managers that their role is not to control people and stay on top of things, but rather to guide, to energize, and to excite.

The CEOs of the best-managed and most profitable companies are listening directly to the people who make the products and serve the customers. They are going out in the field and listening directly to the buyer, who is recognized as the true foundation of corporate power.

To build championship teams, we could take a hint from the legendary football coach from Alabama, Paul "Bear" Bryant, who observed: "I'm just a plowhand from Arkansas, but I've learned how to put and hold a team together. I've learned how to lift some individuals up and how to calm others down, until, finally, they've got one heartbeat as a team. To do that, there's just three things I'd ever have to say: If anything went wrong, I did it. If it went semi-good, then we did it. If anything went real good, then you did it. That's all it takes to get people to win for you."

A new corporate culture that every business and organization must embrace in order to be competitive in the 21st Century is: "To meet ever-increasing customer demands, in rapidly changing world markets, with the highest quality products and services, through educated, skilled, performance-compensated teams who transmit their core excellence and value in their contribution."

List ways you can empower those who depend on you to become winners.

At home: ____

____

At work: ____

____

In your community: ________________________________

____

In what areas of your life can you simplify, delegate and trust?

____

____

Action Thought:
Continuously seek to empower others.
Respond to their needs. Encourage experimentation and tolerate mistakes. Treat every member of your team with equal respect and courtesy.

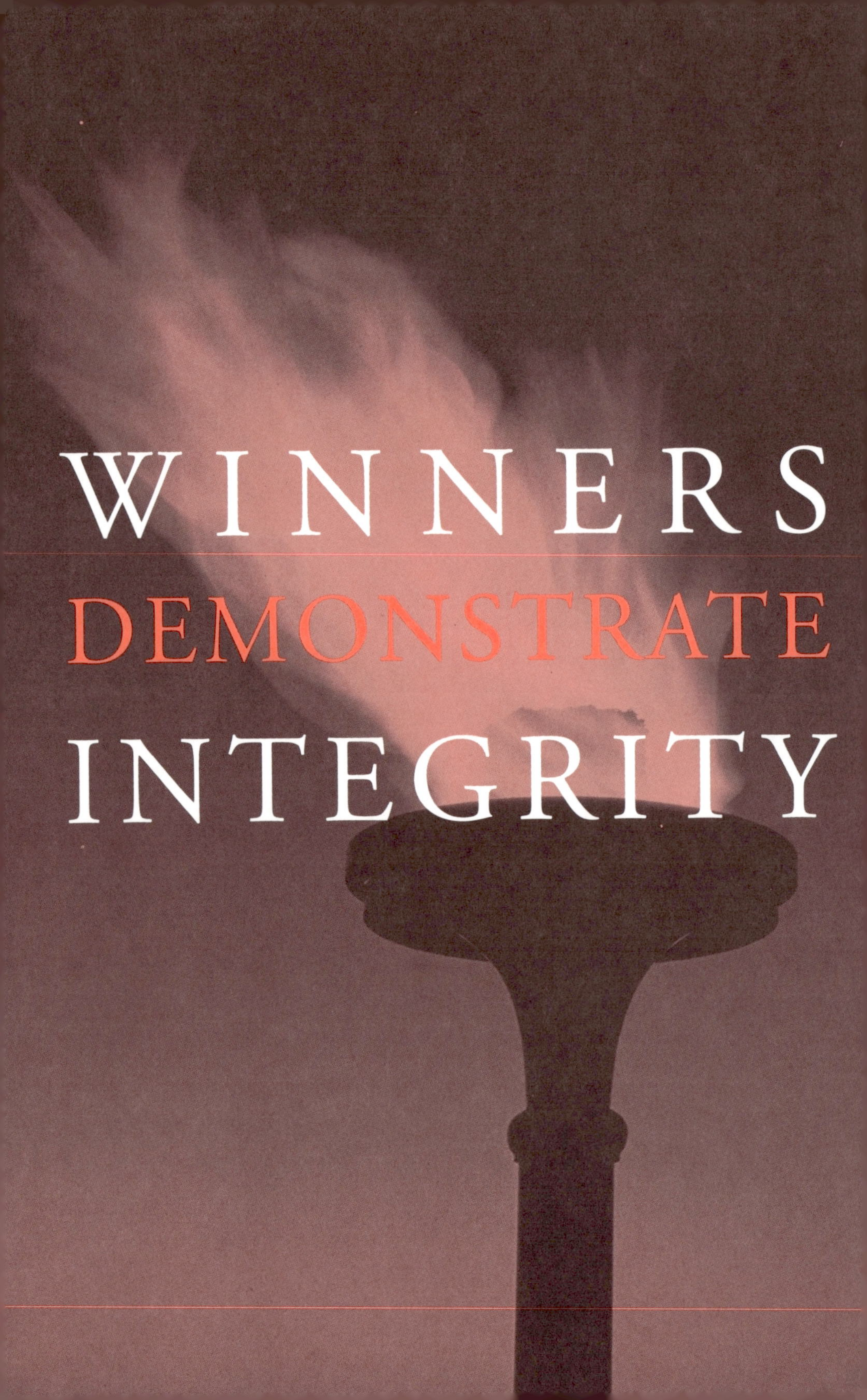
WINNERS
DEMONSTRATE
INTEGRITY

Integrity has a universal meaning. Several decades ago, Madame Chiang Kai-Shek, the first lady and cultural leader of the Chinese people during World War II, put integrity in a golden nutshell when she said: "In the end, we are all the sum total of our actions. Character can't be counterfeited, nor can it be put on and cast off as if it were a garment to meet the whim of the moment. Like the markings on wood which are ingrained in the very heart of the tree, character requires time and nurturing for growth and development."

Integrity that strengthens your inner value system is the real bottom line in every arena. While the popular belief supports the myth that the only thing that counts is bottom line success, the truth is that expediency leads to fleeting stardom and ultimate defeat.

Day by day, we write our own destiny; for inexorably, we become what we do.

Winners are honest in their business and personal relationships. The double standard of having professional and personal lifestyles that don't match is fraudulent. Integrity is not an option. Integrity is a non-situational, absolute standard.

A biting wind tore through the icy slopes on Sarajevo Mountain at the Winter Olympic Games in Yugoslavia. For the Mahre twins, Steve and Phil, this was their last hurrah on the final day of the men's ski competition. Born only minutes apart and always intense competitors, the Mahre twins were in their own private shoot-out for Olympic glory!

Phil Mahre's number came up first and his combined time was good enough to put him in first place for the moment. Still waiting at the top for his second run was Steve Mahre, whose first time left him an excellent shot at the gold.

The normal thing for Phil to do was to wait at the bottom, saying nothing, hoping his time would stand up. Instead he grabbed a walkie-talkie and began radioing advice to Steve on how to ski the course in the fastest time possible.

Although Phil won the gold, even after coaching his brother, Steve still won the silver medal. By getting on that walkie-talkie, Phil had said in so many words to his brother, "If I help you win, I win, too. You may win today, and I tomorrow, but I'm going to give you all my best, because that's what gives me the gold medal within."

Sharing the best of yourself with others is an act of stewardship that makes the world around you more rewarding and enjoyable. When you freely give it as a gift, your integrity inevitably starts a positive chain-reaction in the lives of those who are open to embracing it.

If values are "caught" as well as "taught," how can you be a better role model for the significant adults and children who look to you for guidance?

List examples like healthy habits, safety, generosity and keeping promises.

How can you introduce more integrity in the relationships you have with your family and friends?

Action Thought:
Always think stewardship, teamwork and winning with others. Walk your talk at home and at the office. Be a person with integrity 24 hours a day, 7 days a week.

WINNERS
NEVER STOP
LEARNING

Not long ago, what you learned in school was largely all you needed to learn; you could rely on that knowledge for the rest of your life. With knowledge expanding exponentially, this is no longer true. Hundreds of scientific papers are published daily. Every thirty seconds, some new technological company produces yet another innovation. Your formal education has a very short shelf life, eighteen months at most.

Never again will you be able to go to your place of business on autopilot, comfortable and secure that the organization will provide for and look after you. Knowledge controls access to opportunity and advancement. Scientists and scholars are no longer merely on tap, they are on top. Just as the industrial revolution catered to line managers with manufacturing and materials experience, the knowledge revolution rewards "intellectual entrepreneurs" with strong technical and economic educations.

Three days a week, President Toshifumi Suzuki and his top management have lunch in their boardroom, sampling the instant noodles, prepackaged sandwiches and snacks they plan to sell in their 5,000 store chain. It's a spot check of what's on the shelves. "I won't sell, what I wouldn't eat." says Suzuki.

Backed by some of the most sophisticated product-tracking systems in the world, 7-Eleven Japan is completely tuned in to what customers want. Clerks key in socio-economic and demographic buying patterns at the check-out stand. Orders and customer preferences are transmitted instantly via satellite to distribution centers and manufacturers. Any of the 3,000 items that don't move out of inventory rapidly are discontinued. Its 42 percent operating profit far outshines its competitors.

The 7-Eleven Japan Company is a good example of how 21st Century winners must learn to think. The Japanese firm bought the franchise rights to 7-Eleven from Dallas-based Southland Corporation. By the early 1990s, the franchisee was doing so well it bought control of the American parent. How can a franchisee buy the franchise? By doing its homework.

The definition of power yesterday was defined in natural resources. Today, knowledge is power. With knowledge now the key raw material for creating all economic wealth, the new power struggles will reach deep into our minds and personal lives.

What can you do that will save time and reduce the number of steps necessary to meet your customers'/clients'/organization's needs?

How can you use technology to give you more time to spend with those people most important to you? (i.e. e-mail, internet meetings, teleconferencing, fax dispersal, etc.)

Action Thought:
The acquisition of knowledge is a lifelong experience, not a collection of facts or skill. Consider online education offered by major universities. Read fiction and non-fiction books to increase your vocabulary and knowledge. Constantly upgrade your computer literacy.

WINNERS
NEVER
FINISH

When you ponder why you keep seeking excellence, building and growing throughout your life, remember the cathedral principle. The magnificent cathedrals in Europe, built in centuries past, most often took several lifetimes to design and construct. It was impossible to erect them like office buildings today, in one short period, as if they were Lego blocks. Cathedrals take generations to build. So do great societies, companies and families.

Life is not something to step back from and admire when completed. It is an ongoing process of design, laying the foundations, forming, building bonding, changing, detailing, refining and renovating. We never get it quite right. It is never perfect. It is always under construction.

The continuing nature of the life process and our brief mortal encounter with it calls for the cathedral principle. It calls for us to gain hindsight from all that went before, which is history, with its failures, successes, fashions, and traditions. It calls for us to gain foresight by imagining a better world ahead for all by passing on our trials, errors, and achievements as lessons in leadership. It calls for us to live in the present, longing for neither yesterday nor tomorrow, but rather facing what today offers boldly and enthusiastically.

I was watching the "Today" show one morning and my attention was captured by an interview between Willard Scott and a "Mr. Smith" who was celebrating his 102nd birthday. Mr. Smith had brought his potted plants and was proudly referring to them as his "upstarts."

Willard Scott was becoming frustrated. Time was running out and all Mr. Smith was doing was making a fuss over his chrysanthemums and night-blooming cirrus. "But Mr. Smith," Willard interrupted "we all would really like to know to what you attribute your long life." Mr. Smith, not the least bit senile, went right on touching and watering his flowers, while the audience watched at a hundred and fifty thousand dollars a minute.

"This little lovely won't bloom for another two years," he chuckled, "You want to know my secret for staying active and living so long?" the old man grew serious. "Who would take care of my flowers?"

Perhaps some of the "Today" show viewers got Mr. Smith's point. He might grow flowers that his own eyes would never see in full bloom, but he has just given millions the secret of longevity and fulfillment - for free. Have a purpose that will outlive you! Create something beautiful for others. I went right out and planted a redwood tree and you know how long they live.

Life, like a cathedral, is not so much to be admired for its external appearance and majesty, although these are attractive and noteworthy. Life, like a cathedral, is finding joy in the legacy we are building for future generations.

Life is not a treasure hunt. Life itself is the treasure. It is your collection of memories. Relish your small pleasures and tiny successes. Family reunions. Community service. Intimate moments with a loved one. A baby's first steps. A job well done. Helping a friend. Flying a kite in a good wind. Laughing at something stupid you did. Giving your hand to someone reaching out.

Write down some of the special moments of your life which were spent with someone else.

____

____

____

Have you left a lasting impression on a younger person?

____

____

____

____

Action Thought:
As long as you live, keep learning how to live.

The Psychology of Winning for the 21st Century requires a major paradigm shift in the way we conduct our business and personal lives. There are too many people, too few resources and too delicate a balance between nature and technology to produce winners in isolation today. Instant satellite and internet communications have created a small, global village with blurred borders, few secrets and unparalleled competition.

The new winners in the game of life will act self-employed, while being team leaders capable of empowering others to strive for excellence. From now on, we will be retained and promoted based on the value of our human capitals which includes knowledge, skills, creativity and self-motivation, not on our past education, resume, seniority or position.

Becoming the brand of choice requires confidence, dedication to continuous improvement and total integrity. Because of global competition, the winners will be individuals and organizations who deliver on their promises 24 hours a day, 7 days a week. Winning in the new century is not a destination. It is a way of traveling.

denis  Waitley

Dr. Denis Waitley is recognized as a world authority on high-level achievement and personal excellence. With over 10 million inspirational audio tapes sold in 14 languages, he is the most-listened-to voice on personal and professional development. He is, perhaps best known as the author/narrator of the "The Psychology of Winning," the all-time bestselling non-musical audio program.

Denis is one of the most-sought-after keynote speakers by corporations, associations and institutions in America. Recently, he was named Outstanding Platform Speaker of the Year by the Sales and Marketing Association and inducted into the International Speakers' Hall of Fame. Among his national bestselling books are *The Psychology of Winning, Seeds of Greatness, Being the Best,* and *Empires of the Mind.* He has counseled winners in every field from Superbowl Champions to Apollo Astronauts, from returning POWs from Vietnam, to Fortune 500 top executives. As a member of the U.S. Olympic Committee's sports medicine counsel, he developed a mental training program to enhance the performance of all American Olympic athletes.

Denis is a former Navy pilot, a graduate of the U.S. Naval Academy at Annapolis, and holds a doctorate degree in human behavior.

For information contact:
The Waitley Institute
P.O. Box 197
Rancho Sante Fe, CA 92067

Phone: (619) 756-4201
Fax: (619) 756-9717
e-mail: Denis@DenisWaitley.com
http://www.waitley.com

// The cost is low...
but the ideas are priceless!

Each title in the Successories "Power of One" library takes less than 30 minutes to read, but the wisdom they contain will last a lifetime. Take advantage of volume pricing as you share these insights with all the people who impact your career, your business, your life.

Anatomy of A Leader
This collection of insights written by Carl Mays represents a simple thought-provoking body of knowledge that can help everyone develop the qualities of a leader. #NF713259

Attitude: Your Internal Compass
Denis Waitley and Boyd Matheson give powerful examples of how a slight shift in the way you see the world can yield powerful results in an ever-changing workplace. #NF713193

Burn Brightly Without Burning Out
This book, by motivational expert Dick Biggs, will boost morale and productivity by helping people balance the work they do with the life they lead. #NF716016

Companies Don't Succeed... People Do
Successories founder and Chairman, Mac Anderson, outlines "The Art of Recognition" – how to develop employees and a recognition culture within any organization. #NF716015

Dare to Soar
The spirit of eagles inspired this unique collection of motivational thoughts by noted speaker Byrd Baggett. Any goal can be reached if you "Dare to Soar." #NF716006

The Employee Connection
Noted employee motivation expert Jim Harris provides dozens of practical methods for leaders to "unleash the power of their people." #NF716018

Empowerment
Ken Blanchard and Susan Fowler Woodring's valuable insights into empowerment outlines how to achieve "Peak Performance Through Self-Leadership." #NF716022

Fall In Love with Your Future
Ron and Mary Beshear explore the decisions and life-skills needed to lead a meaningful life. Apply the principles outlined in this refreshing book and begin to take control of your future. #NF716026

Goals
Recognized authority on goal setting, Gary Ryan Blair, outlines tangible guidelines for designing an extraordinary life. His 15 principles, and the "goals workshop," will help you focus on your goals and energize you to propel your life forward! #NF716025

Ignite Your Creative Spark
Rekindle your natural creative spirit as Jordan Ayan provides you with "20 Ways to Fire Up Your Imagination." This book will reveal your hidden potential as it inspires new vistas of creative exploration. #NF716023

Motivating Today's Employees
Recognition expert Bob Nelson offers a great primer on the impact of employee rewards and recognition. #NF716007

Motivating Yourself
Mac Anderson, Successories founder and Chairman, offers a mix of proven ideas and motivational thoughts to help "Recharge the Human Battery." #NF716021

Motivation, Lombardi Style
Use the coach's memorable collection of insights about the athletic playing field and the business battlefield to inspire your team. #NF716013

The Psychology of Winning for the 21st Century
A world authority on high-level achievement and personal excellence, Dr. Denis Waitley provides a unique perspective on what it means to win in the 21st Century. #NF716024

Pulling Together
Nationally-noted author and speaker, John Murphy, outlines "17 Principles for Effective Teamwork" with a refreshing mix of information and thought-provoking questions. #NF716019

Quality, Service, Teamwork
Share these "Foundations of Excellence" with your employees! This valuable resource includes over 100 motivational quotes. #NF716014

Results
Help your sales team turn passion into profit and maximize their relationship power with these proven strategies for changing times. Jeff Blackman's experience and style makes this an entertaining handbook that guarantees results. #NF716017

Rule #One
Author and customer service expert C. Leslie Charles has compiled dozens of insightful ideas, common sense tips and easy-to-apply rules in this customer service handbook. #NF716008

Teamwork
Noted consultant Glenn Parker gives managers, team leaders and members a valuable blueprint for successful team building. Put it to work for your team! #NF716012

Think Change
This intriguing book, by John Murphy, challenges today's employees to change their thinking to keep up with an evolving workplace. "Adapt and Thrive or Fall Behind." #NF716020

To order call toll-free 800-535-2773